TROODON

A MOMENT IN TIME WITH

TROODON

Eric P. Felber, Philip J. Currie
and Jan Sovak

TROODON
PRODUCTIONS INC

Acknowledgement

Only three names appear on the cover as authors and illustrator. However, many other people helped get this book to print. We'd like to say a special thank you to our families who patiently listened to our endless ideas; some of them good, and some of them bad. We'd also like to thank Karen Kryschuk for her help in organizing this book. Her efforts made all of our jobs easier.

To all others who helped, thank you very much.

Eric P. Felber, Philip J.Currie and Jan Sovak

A MOMENT IN TIME WITH TROODON

Text by Eric P. Felber and Philip J. Currie
Illustrations by Jan Sovak
Edited by Laura Purdy Editing Services

COPYRIGHT © 1997 TROODON PRODUCTIONS INC.

"A MOMENT IN TIME" BOOKS ARE PUBLISHED BY
TROODON PRODUCTIONS INC., Suite 1910, 355 4th Avenue S.W.,
Calgary, Alberta T2P OJ1, Canada

CREDITS
Design and cover by Aventinum , Prague
Colour separation and typesetting by Baroa, Prague
Printed and bound by Polygrafprint Prešov
6/02/37/51-01

CANADIAN CATALOGUING IN PUBLICATION DATA

Felber, Eric P. (Eric Peter), 1960-
A moment in time with Troodon

ISBN 0-9682512-0-X

1. Troodon - Juvenile fiction. I. Currie, Philip J..
1949- II. Sovak, Jan, 1953- III. Title

PS8561.E42M64 1997   jC813'.54   C97-900847-6
PZ10.3.F375Mo 1997

PREFACE

*What would a day spent with a family of **Troodon** be like? This book attempts to bring to life a typical day for such a family. Survival is the most basic goal of any animal. This was no different for **Troodon**. Every day presented the challenge of eat or be eaten. Who would be faster today — you or your enemy?*

*Because only partial skeletons of **Troodon** have been found, scientists do not know everything about their anatomy. The most interesting thing that **paleontologists** do know is that **Troodon's** brain was the same size as a modern day ostrich brain. From all information currently available, this size of brain makes **Troodon** the most intelligent of all dinosaurs yet discovered.*

*Fossil sites in Alberta and Montana paint a picture of dinosaur life in the Late Cretaceous period. It was information from these fossil sites that enabled us to write this book. The story, even though a work of fiction, uses the actual scientific information known about **Troodon**. These facts are presented at the end of the story.*

*A **Moment In Time With Troodon** is the beginning of a series of stories. The series will focus on the scientific facts known about specific prehistoric animals. This information will bring a moment in time to life for you.*

TROODON

Morning broke. A faint glimmer of sunlight danced along the still waters of a weed-choked lake. In the distance, a volcano had unleashed its furor, filling the sky with a haze of dull gray ash. Today the sun was having a difficult time breaking through.

A small herd of *Hypacrosaurus* broke the silence of the morning. Noisily, they moved along the edge of the water to feed on the rich vegetation. Not far away, at the top of a small knoll, the tall ferns moved. The sleek, streamlined body of a mother *Troodon* rose from the ground. As she stood, she shook vigorously to remove the thin layer of ash that had coated her body while she slept. She scanned the horizon.

The mother *Troodon* knew that most *predators* searched for their meals before the heat of the afternoon. Therefore, danger was at its peak during the morning hours. *Troodon's* keen senses made it the most alert and cunning of all predators of its time. Using these keen senses, the mother determined that for now, she was safe. She moved down the knoll toward the lake, watching for danger with every step. At the water she lowered her head gently, and took a sip. As she drank, she remained alert to any possible threats.

Her thirst quenched, she stood up and made soft grunting noises. Immediately the vegetation on top of the knoll rustled once again. The ferns parted like a small wave rolling down the knoll. Three juvenile *Troodon* emerged from the vegetation to join their mother by the water's edge. The father *Troodon* stood and shook off his coating of ash. Instincts took

over, and he also scanned the horizon as he walked toward his family. His efforts were not as diligent as the mother's. He knew that if danger was at hand he would have already been alerted by his mate.

At the water's edge, the mother could see that ash was irritating her young ones' eyes. As they walked into the water, the mother used her hand to push them deeper until they became submerged. Thrashing frantically, the little ones were able to get back to the safety of the sandy beach. The irritation they had felt in their eyes was gone.

As with most creatures, the first challenge of the day was to find food. The mother knew that the best places to look for food were the shores of the lake and the river that entered it. She motioned her family north along the shore toward the river.

The river had always been a good source of food for the family. If anything died upstream, there was a reasonable chance that it would be carried downstream to the mouth of the river. This *carrion* supplemented their diet of small lizards, mammals and baby dinosaurs. As the family approached the river, the mother's keen sense of smell let her know that scavenging was not an option in this area. Her nose could sometimes pick up the scent of carrion over a mile away. However, this morning, nothing! Once again, her predatory skills would be put to the test.

The two adults now tuned their senses to living prey. *Troodon*, as one of the smaller predators of the day, relied on hunting smaller animals. If larger prey was available, it had to be young, old or sick. The family set out in search of whatever meal might present itself.

The father *Troodon* walked upstream, skirting the sandy and sometimes muddy edge of the river. The rest of the family followed eagerly. They knew the hunt was on. The juveniles aggressively pushed forward, mimicking their parents, for they had witnessed hunts in the past. The mother let out a grunt, signaling her dissatisfaction with their actions. They were too young and inexperienced to lead a hunt. The young *Troodon* fell back behind their parents, quite proud of their brave actions.

A few yards from the shore of the river, the mother could see the water stirring violently. She stopped and stared. The rest of the family went still. From her expressions and motions they knew she had spotted something. Ever so cautiously, she moved toward the churning water, never taking her eyes off the source of activity. Stepping slowly into the water, she could see a school of fish feeding.

A school of *Myledaphus* had come into the shallows of the river to feed on a bed of clams. *Myledaphus* were well suited for eating clams. Their large, flat-topped teeth could crush the shell in an instant. These fish averaged one to two yards in length.

Grasping such a creature was no easy task for a six foot long dinosaur. The mother knew from experience that the skin of the fish was protected by rows of tiny, tooth-like scales which were rough and unpleasant. She would have to snatch it quickly and throw it onto the sand. She waded to within two yards of the fish, then watched.

Picking a smaller fish would give her better odds for success. She knew she would only have one chance. Waiting patiently, she chose the fish. She leapt forward suddenly, threw her head and shoulders into the water and grasped. Held by the back of the head, the *Myledaphus* flailed frantically, its tail lashing at the mother *Troodon's* neck and back. She turned sideways and flung the fish toward the shore. The father *Troodon* grabbed the tail and dragged the still thrashing fish further onto the sandy beach.

As soon as he was sure the fish could not escape, the father held the *Myledaphus's* head with his right hind foot while the formidable claws of his left foot ripped the fish apart. The adults knew the fish was not enough to fill all of their bellies. They allowed the small *Troodon* to gorge themselves, which they happily did.

When the young had finished, the family began moving farther upstream. Just ahead, lying on the sand, were five or six large dragonflies enjoying the heat of the morning sun. The mother *Troodon* lowered her head, grunted softly, and stared at the dragonflies. The juveniles knew this was their turn to hunt. The adults stood back and watched. Whenever there was an opportunity to let the young ones hunt, the *Troodon* seized the chance for learning. Normal hunting procedure was to move slowly, crouch down, and once close, lunge forward to attack.

But the young ones were impatient. They leapt forward and ran toward their prey. The dragonflies flew into the air over the water. Behind them, the *Troodon* were running and leaping, trying desperately to catch them. The three juveniles, who were

not watching where they were headed, tripped and fell into the water. Standing up, they turned and walked toward their parents. The mother knew how much more the youngsters must learn before they would be successful hunters.

The parents had not yet eaten. With mid morning approaching, satisfying their hunger became a priority. There was a surprising lack of small prey and still no scent of decaying bodies. The day was beginning to grow warm. If they did not find food soon, they would probably have to wait until late afternoon when most animals would be feeding again.

Moving farther upstream, the *Troodon* came upon an old channel that led into the river. It was mostly mud filled with two small ponds of water. The mother *Troodon* noticed some movement between the two pools. Her keen eyesight enabled her to identify it as a turtle. She moved her young into a safe hiding place in the shrubs. Again, just from the mother's motions, the young knew they were to stay still and not move until called upon.

The adults moved toward the muddy bank of the old bend. It was quite steep. Leaning back, the female stepped over the edge and slid down the embankment until she splashed into the water below. The male followed. At the bottom, they both ran toward the murky pools. Here was easy prey. A soft shelled turtle was attempting to get from one watering hole to the next — unfortunate timing for the turtle.

The *Troodon*, knowing that their prey could not get away easily, circled the animal and assessed the situation. They both knew that a turtle bite could yield a very nasty wound.

The mother *Troodon* placed her right foot on top of the turtle's shell, putting on enough pressure so it could not move. The father tried to grab the legs and head of the trapped creature.

The turtle knew its soft exterior was no protection against these predators. All it could do was lie there and wait. The mother applied more pressure on the back of the turtle. Her sickle claw penetrated the shell and pierced the helpless body inside. She turned the turtle on its edge. While she held the shell, the father grasped at the undercarriage and began pulling. In doing so, two of his loose teeth became dislodged and fell to the ground. After a few moments, the upper and lower protective shells ripped apart exposing the soft flesh inside. The two adult *Troodon* quickly consumed the turtle. Be it small, it was a tasty snack.

The adults moved back up the muddy slope to reunite with their young. Midday was approaching and it was time to find a cool spot to rest.

The family found a large growth of ferns. Here the cool, damp shade would provide protection from the blazing sun. They nestled down for the afternoon.

Today was an especially hot day so the family remained in their shady hideaway well into the afternoon. However, with only a few hours of sunlight left, they would have to begin to hunt again. Heading back toward the river was the family's best option. Because of the heat, other animals would be seeking the refuge of the water. At the river, the parents began to search again for potential prey.

All of a sudden, there was movement in some ferns at the edge of the point bar where the *Troodon* were standing! Both parents rushed to investigate, leaving their young at the water's edge.

A small lizard, also seeking a meal, was scampering around the ferns, searching for small bugs and frogs. The lizard, now aware of the danger, frantically ran toward the thicker bushes that lay just ahead. These would give it much more protection from the adult *Troodon* following in hot pursuit.

Meanwhile, the young ones, knowing they had to remain where they were, began playing. The larger of the three moved his head up and down, staring at his two siblings as if they were the prey. This was a game the three often played, mimicking their parents' behavior when they hunted or when they encountered rival *Troodon*.

As the youngsters played, the still water behind them appeared to bulge. The disturbance moved closer, with ripples radiating to the left and right. Unaware of the danger, the small *Troodon* continued their game. Behind them a shadow began to form. The shadow grew, fully covering the young *Troodon*. It grew larger still, extending into the bush. Finally, the largest of the the young ones noticed the presence of a foreign smell. He turned toward the water. Raising his eyes skyward, his muscles tensed. Immediately, he stepped backwards. The others, also sensing danger, turned and looked up.

The long neck and ferocious head of a *plesiosaur* was gazing down upon them. The plesiosaur had seen the *Troodon* at the river's edge, submerged itself, and swam underwater hoping to get as close as possible undetected.

The small *Troodon* began to shriek. As their instincts had taught them, they took up defensive positions and moved back slowly, never taking their eyes off the overpowering creature.

The neck of the plesiosaur moved back. With all the muscles in its neck tense, the head flung forward, its jaws now exposing one to two-inch long needle-sharp teeth. Moving back quickly, the *Troodon* managed to escape the first attack. It was unlikely that the plesiosaur would miss a second time. With the plesiosaur poised and ready to attack again, a second shadow appeared, this time from the opposite direction.

The outstretched body of the mother *Troodon*, her sickle claws extended, latched onto the exposed neck of the plesiosaur. Following directly behind the female was the male *Troodon*. His menacing talons also found their mark. Using their powerful jaws, the *Troodon* held onto the neck and slashed with their two-inch sickle claws, inflicting gaping wounds.

The plesiosaur, its neck thrashing back and forth, threw the *Troodon* to either side of its body. Crashing and rolling to the ground, the adults were quickly back on their feet. They ran and jumped, again latching onto the neck with ferocious determination.

The plesiosaur retreated and slid backward into the water, its neck bleeding profusely. The mother *Troodon* did not want to let go. Her rage at the attack on her children was overwhelming. However, once in the water she knew she

would be no match for this creature. She lashed out one last time, then let go and withdrew to her family.

The wounded plesiosaur, its head limp from the loss of blood, swam as best it could to the other side of the river. Its eyesight, though blurry, was still good enough to see a thirty-foot long *Albertosaurus* breaking through the trees. The *Albertosaurus* had heard the commotion and smelled blood. The plesiosaur knew its strength was gone and could not retreat into the safety of the deeper water.

Seeing the plight of the plesiosaur, the *Albertosaurus* rushed toward the helpless animal. Bending down, it grasped the plesiosaur's neck. Its four-inch serrated teeth severed the head. The *Troodon* family could only watch from afar as the *Albertosaurus* feasted on a meal which could have been theirs.

Three or four birds were now circling overhead. They too were in search of an easy meal. But as long as the *Albertosaurus* was filling itself, the birds could do nothing but wait.

The mother *Troodon* pressed her family to move on, recognizing that darkness would fall in a short time. She knew this area very well. She had hunted here as a youngster with her parents, and many times later as an adult. She remembered that not much further upstream, was a *hadrosaur* nesting site. Herds of hadrosaurs used this area for nesting because it was rich in vegetation. Many forms of edible berries grew there, providing food for the young duck-bill dinosaurs; and the river nearby ensured an ample drinking supply. The

Troodon's idea was simple: move close to the nesting site and hope that some of the young hadrosaurs would stray far enough to provide an easy meal.

The family of *Troodon* moved faster, always close to the river's edge. The mother knew that by following the water she would arrive at the nesting site without getting lost. They came upon a small pool of water and she motioned for the family to take a drink before the last leg of their journey. As they started to drink, the *Troodon* could feel a faint vibration of the ground. Within seconds, small ripples began forming in the pool of water.

The mother stood up, her head turning in all directions. She had experienced this sensation once before, and her instincts told her that danger was close at hand. As she scanned to the west, she could see a cloud of dust in the distance. Amazingly, the dust cloud was at least one mile wide and heading directly toward them.

The mother *Troodon* remembered the last time she had experienced this. As a juvenile, she had watched a stampeding herd of *Anchiceratops* trample and kill her father and one of her siblings. She recalled that the animals had come upon them so quickly that there had been no time to hide.

The landscape to the west was quite open with lots of shrubs and very few trees. But there was one large group of conifers only a few hundred yards away. The mother ran toward the trees and her family followed. The three young *Troodon* never hesitated when they sensed tension in their mother. Seeking out the larger trees, she huddled her children in the middle of four closely packed trunks. They lay still and waited.

The faint vibration soon became a rumble. It seemed the earth was about to shake apart. About one hundred yards from the river's edge was an eight foot high embankment. This drop had been the old river channel's bank.

All of a sudden, like an avalanche, one, ten, fifty, hundreds of stampeding *Anchiceratops* began jumping over the edge of the embankment. The larger, stronger individuals had no trouble reaching the bottom of the drop and continuing on toward the river. Some of the smaller and older ones, however, tried to slow down as they approached the edge of the embankment. The momentum of the herd pushed them over the drop and sent them rolling on their sides. They lay helpless at the bottom and some had no time to get up before being trampled by the herd behind them.

The three-ton animals were now crashing through the trees and shrubs on either side of the *Troodon* family. Luckily the mother had picked a spot where the trees were too close together for the *ceratopsians* to pass.

Without hesitation, the *Anchiceratops* splashed into the river. Fear was in their eyes and escape was clearly their motive. Within minutes, hundreds of the ceratopsians had passed and made their way across the water. Their stampede continued on the other side of the river until all that could be seen of the huge animals was dust.

As the cloud began to settle, an eerie calm pervaded the river's edge. The *Troodon* mother looked toward the embankment where the *Anchiceratops* had stampeded. She could faintly see bodies in the settling dust.

At the base of the small hill lay four corpses. All had been trampled to death. One *Anchiceratops*, barely alive, was trying desperately to stand, but to no avail. The mother *Troodon* sensed the opportunity for food and immediately began moving out of the bush toward the bodies of the *Anchiceratops*. The male was also heading for the mountain of flesh. The parents gave the young ones the signal to stay where they were, at least until they could make sure that no danger existed.

Moving slowly toward the dead animals, the two *Troodon* could detect another presence. Their keen sense of smell picked up a familiar scent, a scent that told them to be cautious.

As they neared the carcasses, the mother sniffed, carefully moving closer. She had to be sure that the *Anchiceratops* were dead before calling her young. The male climbed onto a body and began to bite the side of the dead animal's belly. The *Troodon's* small teeth, even though sharp and serrated, had difficulty penetrating the thick leathery skin of the *Anchiceratops*. Moving his right leg forward, he used his sickle claw to cut and rip a two foot long incision into the belly. Now it was much easier to grasp the flesh and rip off chunks of meat which he swallowed whole.

The mother *Troodon* was uneasy. She could still feel the ground shaking. She moved toward the embankment and began climbing. As her head reached the top, a large male *Albertosaurus* leapt over the embankment, landing twenty feet behind her. The leap barely interrupted the beast's stride

as it rushed to the river's edge. It was now obvious why the stampede had started.

The *Albertosaurus* was about to enter the river to resume the pursuit when the one surviving *Anchiceratops* at the base of the embankment let out two desperate grunts. The head of the *Albertosaurus* turned toward the sound. In the chase, he had not even noticed the carcasses at the base of the embankment. The *carnivore* quickly turned and headed toward the bodies.

The two *Troodon* slowly backed away from the feast. The *Albertosaurus* noticed their movement and made offensive, warning gestures toward them. He knew they posed no threat and so he allowed the *Troodon* to make their retreat. The huge carnivore then made his way to the still moving *Anchiceratops* and sent his left leg crashing down on its belly. Using his jaws, the *Albertosaurus* grasped the neck and held on until all motion stopped.

The mother *Troodon* knew there might still be an opportunity to feed since there were four other carcasses lying there. However, she also knew it took more than one *Albertosaurus* to stampede hundreds of ceratopsians. She looked up and saw five more *Albertosaurus* standing on the embankment.

The *Troodon* moved hastily toward the security of the trees where they had left their young. From the trees they could only watch as again, an easy meal disappeared. The mother *Troodon* stared as the tyrannosaurs feasted and she knew they would probably spend most of the day filling their bellies. She could not wait that long to eat; the family was too hungry now.

They continued their journey up river toward the hadrosaur breeding grounds. In the distance they could hear the faint grunts of many hadrosaurs, and knew they were getting close. As they neared the nesting site, the sky turned a light orange. Dusk approached and darkness would soon follow.

The *Troodon* family, now only a few hundred yards away from the nesting site, made their way into the thick marsh vegetation. The young were again forced to lie still and wait. Moving toward the nesting site, the adult *Troodon* picked up a different scent. They sensed it belonged to a distantly related predator.

Moving cautiously, they came to a small opening. It was a trail that split the marsh in half. This was the hadrosaurs' path to the river and led directly to the nesting site. With barely an eye peering out from behind the thick vegetation, the female *Troodon* could now see the nesting site. The hadrosaurs were busily preparing for nightfall.

The nesting site was situated two hundred feet from the river. It was a perfect spot, on top of a small flattened hill. Surrounded by rich vegetation, it provided ample food for the hadrosaurs and their young. Four-foot marsh sedges as well as a few cycads and coniferous trees surrounded the hill.

With dusk fast approaching, almost all the adults were back in the nesting colony. The colony was extremely active. Adults moved between the nests and the babies loudly demanded to be fed their last meal of the day. Some of the young were nearly three weeks old and weighed twenty pounds. Growing up fast was essential to their survival.

The mother *Troodon* noticed some movement about twenty yards toward the colony on the other side of the path. Her keen sense of smell had been right. There were other predators in the area. A *Dromaeosaurus* head emerged from the vegetation on the other side of the path. Fortunately, the *Troodon* were downwind from the *dromaeosaur* and he had not picked up their scent.

Dromaeosaurus was a more robust predator than *Troodon* and stood about five feet tall. It was almost eight feet long, and had slender, razor-like teeth. Although the adult *Troodon* were smaller, they were also sleeker, faster and more maneuverable than their competitor. But the female *Troodon* knew that *Dromaeosaurus* hunted in packs, which made them a formidable opponent.

Movement of the vegetation beside the *Dromaeosaurus* announced the appearance of three more animals. The mother *Troodon* slowly crouched, not wanting to be noticed. She would wait for the cover of darkness in order to slip away. As evening approached, the irises of her large eyes opened wider to absorb what little light remained. She could see that the dromaeosaurs were stalking the colony. They too were waiting for nightfall.

In the lengthening shadows, the young *Troodon* stretched out quietly among the exposed roots of a cypress. No sound passed between them, but their large eyes watched alertly for any movement from the direction of the dromaeosaurs. Because they were downwind, they could detect the dromaeosaurs' slightly acrid odor, familiar, but different from

their own. The odor sharpened in the gathering darkness as tension caught hold of the predators. They would attack soon.

The hadrosaurs were not entirely oblivious to their danger. The large bulls at the edge of the herd were facing the forest and occasionally lifted their heads to sample the air for scents. The hadrosaurs may have detected a hint of danger in the gentle breeze. But the air was heavy with the soothing aroma of flowering trees and moist undergrowth. The hadrosaurs peered into the growing darkness. Their eyesight was good in the daylight, and their field of vision was very wide. However, in the twilight gloom, these beasts were easily confused by any movement. Even they did not trust what they saw.

The two adult *Troodon* rose quietly from their haunches when they detected movement across the trail. Their young remained on the ground, dutifully watching the adults even as the dromaeosaurs emerged from the underbrush. One of the big bull hadrosaurs caught sight of the slowly approaching pack, and let out a trumpeting bellow to warn the colony.

The dromaeosaurs did not rush toward the giant bulks. What would have been the point of that? The herd was surrounded by an open area where the hungry *herbivores* had stripped the leaves and twigs from the lowest branches of the trees. All of the undergrowth had been ripped up or trampled leaving no place for the dromaeosaurs to hide. As fast as they were, the dromaeosaurs could not hope to cover this intervening space fast enough to catch the hadrosaurs unaware. So they simply walked cautiously toward the bellowing, moving wall of flesh. More hadrosaurs from the herd were rapidly closing all the gaps. The dromaeosaurs stopped to assess the situation.

The young *Troodon* rose when their mother looked at them each in turn. They had been watching for this signal. The wait was over. As the confrontation escalated between the dromaeosaurs and the hadrosaurs, the *Troodon* moved deeper into the woods, angling away from the nesting grounds toward the river.

Reaching the bank, they dropped over the edge and traveled beside the river toward the center of the colony. Several bulls were sitting on the ridge above them, but were facing their comrades who were holding the dromaeosaurs at bay. By now the whole herd was aroused, and was sending up a terrible din. The adults bellowed warnings at the predators and grunted commands to their young who were squealing nervously in the nests.

The *Troodon* climbed the bank, and slipped behind the tangled roots of a giant cypress. The tree had toppled during the last flood and its trunk had been carried downstream to its current resting position. It lay across the crest of the river's natural *levee*, with its crown deeply imbedded in mud and sand.

The young *Troodon* trembled slightly as they gazed on the enormous colony that extended as far as they could see. They choked back the urge to gag at the overpowering odor of feces, urine, half digested food and decomposing bodies that assailed their delicate nostrils. All of the refuse, including dead hatchlings, was pushed into the walkways. Along these paths, two adults could comfortably pass each other without fear of stepping over the raised margins of the nests. It was an imposing sight; one that the adult *Troodon* had experienced more than a dozen times when the hadrosaurs came through on their annual migrations.

The huge red moon rose as though it was being squeezed through a hole in the forest floor. Ominous moonlight enveloped the battleground and the dromaeosaurs began to make their move. One by one, they started running at the semi-circle of bulls that separated them from the young. Until now, no animal on either side was in danger. But the game of thrust and feint was one of skill and patience. These are two qualities often lacking in the young of all species. Sooner or later, someone would make a mistake.

One of the younger dromaeosaurs came in too close, overconfident in the intoxicating knowledge of his own agility and speed. At three years old, he was coming into his prime. He was still smaller and lighter than the older males, and his legs were relatively longer. As he charged toward the hadrosaurs, one of the young bulls broke ranks and surged forward to intercept him.

The male dromaeosaur reversed direction immediately, but one of his female comrades was following so close that she did not see the danger soon enough. As she tried to change direction, she slipped in a pile of fresh, slimy manure. The young hadrosaur bore down on the hapless predator like a meteor.

Before the smaller animal could regain her footing, she was hit broadside with a foot propelled by four tons of angry

resentment. Her slender ribs snapped like toothpicks. A mixed foam of blood and air was expelled from her lungs through her mouth and nostrils. She was dead before she hit the ground. Still, the hadrosaur charged after her with eyes oblivious to all else that was happening. Within seconds the giant padded feet had reduced the carcass to a shapeless mass on the ground.

Only then did the bull become conscious of a sharply increasing pain in his side. He turned to see the young male dromaeosaur slipping to the ground. It was too late. The damage was done. For a short time, the hadrosaur had exposed his unprotected flanks. The predator had seized the opportunity to attack .

Again, the dromaeosaur leapt high in the air sinking his front talons deep into the thick hide. The carnivore's body went rigid. He stretched to full length, driving both raptorial claws between the ribs of the hadrosaur. Without hesitation the dromaeosaur dropped toward the ground, his terrible claws slicing the hadrosaur's flesh with surgical precision. While he tore through the belly of the giant, the raptor pushed hard against the bloodied wall with his arms, twisting his body as he dropped to the ground.

As soon as his feet touched the moist earth, his muscular legs shot him into the air again, propelling him away from what was otherwise certain death. The end of the hadrosaur's thick tail caught him with a glancing blow to the left hip, sending him cartwheeling across the clearing. Without thinking of the pain, he rolled onto his feet and moved behind one of the trees.

Bruised but alive, the carnivore turned to look on a scene of pandemonium. The remaining dromaeosaurs smelled the blood of their dead comrade and the isolated hadrosaur. They focused all their fury on the wounded giant. The young bull had charged too far from the protection of the older and wiser bulls. They would not risk breaching their lines of defense, even though other animals were moving up to strengthen those lines. Bleeding from dozens of long, vertical wounds, the unfortunate bull attempted to return to the herd. He collapsed on the ground, only a few body lengths short of his goal. The predators no longer heeded the stares and bellows of the other bulls. They leapt on the downed animal, his eyes glazing.

By the time the victorious predators started to feed on the still quivering mountain of flesh, the hadrosaurs were pulling slowly back toward the nests. They sensed that the dromaeosaurs had what they wanted, and would bother them no more.

At the onset of the dromaeosaur attack, the Troodon had broken cover and charged into the core of the colony. Few animals could equal them in speed. Their cousins the *ornithomimids* were faster, but were timid predators whose toothless, beaked jaws were feared only by lizards, mammals and other small creatures.

Some of the hadrosaurs bellowed loudly as the *Troodon* ran a torturous course between their pillar-like legs. But in the poor light, most were oblivious to the intruders. Their sense of smell was dulled by the stench of the colony, and their attention was diverted by the commotion near the margin of the forest.

The target of the little family of predators was an unprotected nest not far from the river. Almost twenty recently hatched babies were peeking over the mounded edge of the nest. They were looking for the mother who had left the colony early in the day to search for food, or the father who stood with the other bulls protecting the young from the dromaeosaurs.

The babies' instinct was to stay within the nest. Here they would not be trampled by the adults who were more than a thousand times their weight. This instinct was so strong that none of the hatchlings attempted to flee when the female *Troodon* catapulted over the top of their nest. Half were dead before the male predator and his *progeny* leaped into the depression.

If the neighboring hadrosaurs were aware of the presence of the pack, they showed no sign of alarm as the *Troodon* settled down on their haunches to enjoy their grisly feast. By the time the bull returned to his nest, the predators had left, carrying off the uneaten young and leaving only a few of their loose teeth as calling cards.

Dawn found the family of *Troodon* far from the nesting colony of the hadrosaurs. The young still slept in a tightly woven ball of necks, tails, and limbs. The female stretched languidly as rays from the early morning sun filtered down through the forest canopy. Her mate turned his alert gaze toward her. Did his eyes hold a trace of admiration for her prowess? Perhaps.

What do we really know about *Troodon*?

Troodon was a small carnivorous dinosaur belonging to the family troodontidae, whose known members also include *Borogovia*, *Saurornithoides*, *Sinornithoides*, and *Tochisaurus*. *Troodon* was described in 1856, making it one of the earliest dinosaurs discovered in North America. Unfortunately, the first known specimen was only a single tooth.

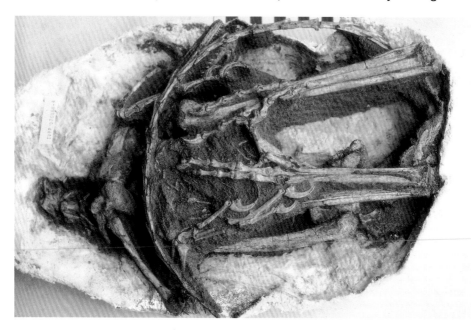

IVPP07088 - 4 Beautifully preserved skeleton of *Sinornithoides*, an animal closely related to *Troodon*. *(Photograph by Philip Currie.)*

It was very distinctive — a small tooth with serrations larger than those of the gigantic *Tyrannosaurus rex*. Scientists speculated about what *Troodon* looked like for more than a century. Some thought it was a lizard. Some identified it as a plant-eating dinosaur now known as the dome-headed *Stegoceras*. But most assigned it to various groups of carnivorous dinosaurs.

In 1983, Dr. Jack Horner was visiting me in Drumheller. While we were walking in the badlands behind the Royal Tyrrell Museum of Palaeontology, he found a lower jaw with teeth in it. This was the link needed to associate the teeth with various parts of the skeleton. Although no complete skeleton had ever been found, partial skeletons had been recovered, all of them lacking teeth. Today, thanks to that discovery in the badlands of the Red Deer River, we know what practically the whole skeleton looks like.

The body weight of this small, slender dinosaur was only about 100 pounds (45 kilograms). In total length, *Troodon* was about 6 feet (l.75 meters) from the tip of the nose to the tip of the tail. Distantly related to the ostrich-mimic dinosaurs (ornithomimids), it was an animal built to run very rapidly. The legs were relatively long, and the lower parts of the leg were especially elongated. We walk on the flats (soles) of our feet, but troodontids stood on their toes like most other dinosaurs. However, only two toes actually touched the ground when this animal was running. The third toe that normally touches the ground had developed an enlarged, highly curved and sharply pointed claw. To keep the claw sharp, troodontids had to carry it off the ground. In this respect, troodontids were similar to the "raptors" (dromaeosaurs). The claw was probably used to capture prey.

6516 Skull of *Saurornithoides*, another member of the *Troodon* family. *(Photograph by Philiph Currie.)*

Reconstruction of a *Troodon* head in which real teeth were used.
(Photograph by Lawrence Dohy.)

Troodon was clearly a sharp-toothed, sharp-clawed, meat-eating theropod. However, the teeth are numerous and small, so it probably did not eat the same things as the bone-crunching tyrannosaurs. Scientists have been able to speculate about *Troodon's* feeding habits by examining fossil sites.

Recently, three sites have been found near Drumheller where the most common fossil is *Troodon* teeth. These teeth were "baby teeth" that were lost when new ones grew in. The high number of teeth found at these locations suggests that these places were feeding sites. Unlike mammals, dinosaurs replaced their teeth constantly as long as they lived. With more than a hundred teeth in its jaws, each of which was replaced every two years, a troodontid lost a few rootless crowns every time it fed.

The second most common fossils at the sites where the *Troodon* teeth are found, are bones from baby duck-billed dinosaurs. This suggests that troodontids may have fed on hadrosaurs when they hatched from their eggs. Another significant find at one site was a large quantity of dromaeosaur teeth. This discovery would indicate that these two predators were probably in competition for food at this location.

At one site near Jenner, Alberta, a full turtle shell with a small indentation on the top was found. Within one foot of the fossil were two *Troodon* teeth. Could a *Troodon* have bitten into the shell and lost two of its teeth? Could the formidable sickle claw of a *Troodon* have left its mark on the top of the turtle shell?

The eyes of *Troodon* were very large, and because they faced forward in their sockets, they had overlapping fields of vision. This

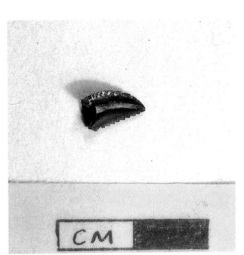

Typically serrated tooth of *Troodon*.
(Photograph by Lawrence Dohy.)

suggests that they could see in three dimensions like humans. Most plant-eating dinosaurs had eyes that were more widely spaced and could not see in stereo. This difference between the two types of dinosaurs is easy to explain. Hunters need more precise vision in order to strike more

Two *Troodon* teeth were found beside this turtle shell.
(Photograph by Eric Felber.)

accurately at prey and manipulate their food. Plant eaters, however, need to have the widest field of vision possible to give them an early warning of the approach of a carnivore. The large eyes of *Troodon* might also indicate that it did most of its hunting at night.

More information about *Troodon's* hunting behavior has been found at a location in Montana. This site contains the remains of many individual *Troodon*, from half grown "teenagers" to full adults. The presence of many individuals in one place is a line of evidence that scientists have used to establish herding or packing behavior. *Troodon* probably hunted in groups.

Authors Eric P. Felber and Philip J. Currie standing above *Troodon* fossil site. *(Photograph by Eva Koppelhus.)*

Scientists can also speculate about *Troodon's* life span. By looking at the microscopic structure of the bones, we can see that *Troodon* was a rapidly growing dinosaur that lived for about two decades.

Another aspect of *Troodon's* anatomy, which has attracted a great deal of attention, is its possible relationship to the earliest known birds. Although not directly ancestral to birds, *Troodon* is anatomically close enough to these modern flying dinosaurs to establish their relationship.

Perhaps the most remarkable feature of *Troodon*, however, is its large brain. Paleontologists sometimes find skulls that are so well preserved that the shape of the brain is retained. By pouring liquid rubber into the hole where the spinal cord comes out, a replica of the brain can be pulled out when it dries. Scientists can then measure it, calculate how much it weighed in comparison with the animal's body weight, and compare it mathematically with modern animals. *Troodon* had a brain that was about six times larger than the brain of a crocodile of the same body weight. This suggests that *Troodon* was much more intelligent than a crocodile and might have been as bright as some modern mammals and birds.

Over the last decade, *Troodon* has become one of the more popular dinosaurs because so many interesting things have been discovered about it. Still, there are many more mysteries waiting to be solved about this fascinating animal.

Illustrator Jan Sovak.
(Photograph by Daniela Sovak.)

GLOSSARY

Albertosaurus: "Alberta lizard"; a type of meat-eating dinosaur related to *Tyrannosaurus rex.*; first discovered in 1884 near the present city of Drumheller, Alberta, Canada.

Anchiceratops: "Similar horned face"; a plant-eating horned dinosaur from the Late Cretaceous; found in Alberta.

carnivore: any meat-eater, from fish to birds and mammals.

carrion: the meat of a dead animal; carcass.

ceratopsians: "Horned faced" dinosaurs; plant-eating, bird-hipped dinosaurs that lived during the Late Cretaceous period, from about 100 until 65 million years ago; characterized by horns on the face and a frill that extends from the back of the skull over the neck.

coniferous: "Evergreen" trees belonging to the order Coniferales (cone-bearing trees).

cycad: a gymnosperm (a seed plant in which the seeds are not enclosed in an ovary); looks like a palm but belongs to an entirely different order (Cycadales) which is the second largest order of living gymnosperms; today they grow in tropical and subtropical parts of the world.

cypress: an evergreen coniferous tree; branchlets are densely covered with small, overlapping, scale-like, decussate leaves.

dromaeosaur: "Swift lizard"; a theropod; fast running meat-eating dinosaur.

hadrosaur: the duck-billed dinosaurs; a group of plant-eating animals that were very successful at the end of the Cretaceous period.

herbivore: plant-eater.

Hypacrosaurus: "Very high ridged lizard"; one of the duck-billed dinosaurs (hadrosaurs); fossils of eggs, embryos, hatchlings, juveniles and adults have been found in Alberta and Montana.

levee: a ridge that forms the banks of a river that is close to sea-level.

Myledaphus: a clam-eating ray fish from the Late Cretaceous; found in the northern hemisphere.

ornithomimid: "Bird mimic"; a family of fast, long-legged theropods that had lost their teeth and developed a toothless bill.

paleontologist: a scientist specialized in the study of prehistoric life; the study of fossil plants or animals.

plesiosaur: "Near lizards" are not dinosaurs, but are marine reptiles that lived in the seas and grew almost as large as dinosaurs.

predator: a meat-eating animal that hunts and kills its prey.

progeny: children, or descendants.

raptor: "Thief or robber"; a name that is used for predatory birds like hawks and eagles, and for some of the small, meat-eating dinosaurs like dromaeosaurs and *Troodon*.